Building
Character
in Your Children

By Crawford and Karen Loritts

*"Unless the Lord
builds the house,
its builders
labor in vain"*
(Psalm 127:1a).

FAMILYLIFE™
Bringing Timeless Principles Home
Little Rock, Arkansas

Loveland, Colorado

Group resources actually work!

This Group resource helps you focus on **"The 1 Thing™"**— a life-changing relationship with Jesus Christ. "The 1 Thing" incorporates our **R.E.A.L.** approach to ministry. It reinforces a growing friendship with Jesus, encourages long-term learning, and results in life transformation, because it's:

Relational
Learner-to-learner interaction enhances learning and builds Christian friendships.

Experiential
What learners experience through discussion and action sticks with them up to 9 times longer than what they simply hear or read.

Applicable
The aim of Christian education is to equip learners to be both hearers and doers of God's Word.

Learner-based
Learners understand and retain more when the learning process takes into consideration how they learn best.

Visit our Web site: **www.grouppublishing.com**

Credits
FamilyLife
Editor: David Boehi

Group Publishing, Inc.
Editor: Matt Lockhart
Chief Creative Officer: Joani Schultz
Copy Editor: Christy Fagerlin
Art Directors: Jenette L. McEntire, Jean Bruns, and Randy Kady
Print Production Artist: Spearhead, Inc.
Cover Art Director: Jeff A. Storm
Cover Designer: Alan Furst, Inc.
Cover Photographer: Daniel Treat
Illustrator: Ken Jacobson
Production Manager: Peggy Naylor

ISBN 0-7644-2552-8
10 9 8 7 6 5 4 3 2 1   13 12 11 10 09 08 07 06 05 04

Printed in the United States of America.

How to Let the Lord Build Your House
and not labor in vain

The HomeBuilders Parenting Series®: A small-group
Bible study dedicated to making your family all that God
intended.

FamilyLife is a division of Campus Crusade for Christ International, an evangelical Christian organization founded in 1951
by Bill Bright. FamilyLife was started in 1976 to help fulfill the
Great Commission by strengthening marriages and families and
then equipping them to go to the world with the gospel of Jesus
Christ. The Weekend to Remember conference is held in most
major cities throughout the United States and is one of the
fastest-growing marriage conferences in America today. "FamilyLife Today," a daily radio program hosted by Dennis Rainey,
is heard on hundreds of stations across the country. Information
on all resources offered by FamilyLife may be obtained by contacting us at the address, telephone number, or World Wide
Web site listed below.

Dennis Rainey, Executive Director
FamilyLife
P.O. Box 8220
Little Rock, AR 72221-8220
1-800-FL-TODAY
www.familylife.com

FamilyLife™
Bringing Timeless Principles Home

A division of Campus Crusade for Christ International
Bill Bright, Founder
Steve Douglass, President

About the Sessions

Each session in this study is composed of the following categories: Warm-Up, Blueprints, Wrap-Up, and HomeBuilders Project. A description of each of these categories follows:

Warm-Up (15 minutes)

The purpose of Warm-Up is to help people unwind from a busy day and get to know each other better. Typically the first point in Warm-Up is an exercise that is meant to be fun while introducing the topic of the session. The ability to share in fun with others is important in building relationships. Another component of Warm-Up is the Project Report (except in Session One), which is designed to provide accountability for the Home-Builders Project that is to be completed by couples between sessions.

Blueprints (60 minutes)

This is the heart of the study. In this part of each session, people answer questions related to the topic of study and look to God's Word for understanding. Some of the questions are to be answered by couples, in subgroups, or in the group at large. There are notes in the margin or instructions within a question that designate these groupings.

Wrap-Up (15 minutes)

This category serves to "bring home the point" and wind down a session in an appropriate fashion.

HomeBuilders Project (60 minutes)

This project is the unique application step in a HomeBuilders study. Before leaving a meeting, couples are encouraged to "Make a Date" to do the project for the session prior to the next meeting. Most HomeBuilders Projects contain three sections: (1) As a Couple—a brief exercise designed to get the date started, (2) Individually—a section of questions for husbands and wives to answer separately, and (3) Interact as a Couple—an opportunity for couples to share their answers with each other and to make application in their lives.

Another feature you will find in this course is a section of Parent-Child Interactions. There is a corresponding interaction for each session. These interactions provide parents an excellent opportunity to communicate with their children on the important topics covered in this course.

In addition to the above regular features, occasional activities are labeled "For Extra Impact." These are activities that generally provide a more active or visual way to make a particular point. Be mindful that people within a group have different learning styles. While most of what is presented is verbal, a visual or active exercise now and then helps engage more of the senses and appeals to people who learn best by seeing, touching, and doing.

About the Authors

Crawford and Karen Loritts are speakers and writers with Campus Crusade for Christ, where Crawford also serves as associate director of U.S. Ministries. They met as students at Philadelphia College of Bible (now called Philadelphia Biblical University), and worked several years as speakers and church planters.

In 1982, Crawford founded Here's Life Black America (HLBA), a ministry of Campus Crusade. Its purpose was to impact individuals, particularly leaders, in the black community to help rebuild the spiritual heritage upon which many of its institutions were established. In the summer of 1991, Here's Life Black America changed its name to Legacy. The major focus of Legacy is to act as a catalyst in helping to rebuild and restore strong, God-honoring families in Urban America.

Crawford served as co-chair of the 1997 National Congress on the Urban Family. He is in demand as a speaker at conferences (including Promise Keepers); churches; conventions; and various colleges, universities, and seminaries. His speaking engagements have taken him across the United States, to Canada, Europe, Africa, Asia, and the Caribbean. He and Karen also serve on the speaker team for FamilyLife's Weekend to Remember conferences.

Crawford has a radio program, "Living a Legacy" with FamilyLife, and has served on many boards and advisory committees. As an author, he has written four books: *A Passionate Commitment*, *Never Walk Away*, *Make It Home Before Dark*, and *Lessons From a Life Coach*. He has a Doctor of Divinity degree from Biola University, a Doctor of Sacred Theology degree from Philadelphia Biblical University, and a Doctor of Letters from Trinity International University. He and Karen have four children and make their home near Atlanta.

Contents

Acknowledgments

This study is the product of the love, encouragement, and help of some very special people...A special thanks goes to our dear friend, Dennis Rainey, who asked us to write this study several years ago. We also want to thank FamilyLife for the partnership we have enjoyed now for more than twenty years. In a very real sense these pages are a result of that wonderful relationship.

And what can we say about Dave Boehi! Thanks, Dave, for your perseverance and for shaping this material and putting it into "readable form." We could not have done this without you. You are a gifted writer and a great friend. We love and appreciate you.

We are also grateful to the team at Group Publishing for their commitment to this project and for working with us in pulling this together.

Thank you for taking this study. It is our prayer that God will use this study to equip and encourage you in the important task of shaping this and future generations!

Introduction

Nearly all of the important jobs in our culture require intensive training. We would not think of allowing someone to practice medicine, for example, without first attending medical school and completing a residency.

But do you realize that most people receive little training in how to fulfill one of the most important responsibilities of our lives—being effective parents? When we bring a new life into the world, we burst with pride and joy…but are often ignorant of how to actually raise that child to become a mature, responsible adult.

In response to the need we see in families today, FamilyLife and Group Publishing have developed a series of small-group studies called the HomeBuilders Parenting Series. These studies focus on raising children and are written so that parents of children of all ages will benefit.

For these HomeBuilders studies, we have several goals in mind: First, *we want to encourage you in the process of child rearing*. We feel that being a mom or a dad is a high calling and an incredible privilege. We also know how easy it is to feel overwhelmed by the responsibility, especially when you have young children. Participating in a HomeBuilders group can connect you with other parents who share your struggles. The help and encouragement you receive from them will be invaluable.

Second, *we want to help you develop a practical, biblical plan for parenting*. It's so easy for parents to take parenting one day at a time. But as we've raised our children, we've learned that we need to understand biblical guidelines on parenting and then make proactive plans on how we will apply them.

Third, *we want to enhance and strengthen your teamwork as a couple*. You will learn together how to apply key biblical truths, and in the HomeBuilders Projects you will talk through how to apply them to your unique family situation. In the process, you will have the opportunity to discuss issues that you may have ignored or avoided in the past. And you'll spend time regularly in prayer, asking God for his direction and power.

Fourth, *we want to help you connect with other parents so you can encourage and help one another*. You could complete this study with just your spouse, but we strongly urge you to either form or join a group of couples studying this material. You will find that the questions in each study will help create a special environment of warmth, encouragement, and fellowship as you meet together to study how to build the type of home you desire. You will have the opportunity to talk with other parents to learn some new ideas…or to get their advice…or just to see that others are going through the same experiences. Participating in a HomeBuilders group could be one of the highlights of your life.

Finally, *we want to help you strengthen your relationship with God*. Not only does our loving Father provide biblical principles for parenting, but our relationship with him allows us to rely on his strength and wisdom. In fact, it is when we feel most powerless and inadequate as parents that he is most real to us. God loves to help the helpless parent.

The Bible: Blueprints for Building Your Family

You will notice as you proceed through this study that the Bible is used frequently as the final authority on issues of life, marriage, and parenting. Although written thousands of years ago, this Book still speaks clearly and powerfully about the struggles we face in our families. The Bible is God's Word—his blueprint for building a God-honoring home and for dealing with the practical issues of living.

We encourage you to have a Bible with you for each session. For this series we use the New International Version as our primary reference. Another excellent translation is the New American Standard Bible.

A Special Word to Single Parents

Although the primary audience for this study is married couples, we recognize that single parents will benefit greatly from the experience. If you are a single parent, you will find that some of the language and material does not apply directly to you. But most of what you will find in this study is timeless wisdom taken directly from Scripture and can help you develop a solid, workable plan for your family. We hope you will be flexible and adapt the material to your specific situation.

If possible, you might want to attend the group sessions with another single parent. This will allow you to encourage each other and hold each other accountable to complete the HomeBuilders Projects.

Ground Rules

Each group is designed to be enjoyable and informative— and non-threatening. Three simple ground rules will help ensure that everyone feels comfortable and gets the most out of the experience.

1. Don't share anything that would embarrass your spouse or violate the trust of your children.

2. You may pass on any question you don't want to answer.

3. If possible, plan to complete the HomeBuilders Project as a couple between group sessions.

A Few Quick Notes About Leading a Home-Builders Group

1. Leading a group is much easier than you may think! A group leader in a HomeBuilders session is really a "facilitator." As a facilitator, your goal is simply to guide the group through the discussion questions. You don't need to teach the material—in fact, we don't want you to! The special dynamic of a HomeBuilders group is that couples teach themselves.

2. This material is designed to be used in a home study, but it also can be adapted for use in a Sunday school environment. (See pages 119-120—"In a Sunday school class"—for more information about this option.)

3. We have included a section of Leader Notes in the back of this book. Be sure to read through these notes before leading a session; they will help you prepare.

4. For more material on leading a HomeBuilders group, get a copy of the *HomeBuilders Leader Guide* by Drew and Kit Coons. This book is an excellent resource that provides helpful guidelines on how to start a study, how to keep discussion moving, and much more.

What Legacy Are You Leaving?

Your life will have an impact for generations to come.

W A R M • U P   15 M I N U T E S

Trials and Triumphs

Introduce yourself, and tell the group the names and ages of your children. Then choose one or two of the following questions to respond to.

- What, to you, is the best thing about being a parent right now?

- What is the most difficult thing about being a parent right now?

- What is something you have that has been passed down to you from your parents or grandparents?

- What are you hoping to get out of participating in this group?

Getting Connected

Pass your books around the room, and have everyone write in their names, phone numbers, and e-mail addresses.

_____

NAME, PHONE, AND E-MAIL

_____

NAME, PHONE, AND E-MAIL

_____

NAME, PHONE, AND E-MAIL

_____

NAME, PHONE, AND E-MAIL

_____

NAME, PHONE, AND E-MAIL

_____

NAME, PHONE, AND E-MAIL

BLUEPRINTS   6o MINUTES

If you have a large group, form smaller groups of about six people to answer the Blueprints questions. Unless otherwise noted, answer the questions in your subgroup. Before moving on to the Wrap-Up section, have sub-groups report to the whole group the highlights from their discussions.

What We Leave Behind

The American Heritage Dictionary (Second College Edition) defines _legacy_ as "something handed down from an ancestor or predecessor or from the past." You can receive a legacy from many different people in your life, but the most important place for a legacy to be passed on is within a family.

1. Who are two or three people who have had a significant and positive impact in your life? Write their names down along with a brief description of what type of impact each of these people has had on your life.

2. Choose one of the people on your list, and tell the group one way this person has had a positive influence in your life.

3. How have you seen the following statement to be true?
"All parents leave some type of legacy with their children—whether they intend to or not."

4. When people think of the legacy they received from their parents, do you think they usually tend to focus most on the *type of people their parents are* (or were) or on their *financial success* or on their *outward accomplishments*? Explain.

Focusing on Character

The impact of your life will be felt for generations to come. It is so easy to get caught up in the struggles and pressures of surviving and raising a family in today's world that we forget that the life you live is your real legacy. Your values, your convictions, your priorities—in other words, your *character*—will influence your children…and their children…and their children.

5. When you think of someone who has "good character," what does that mean to you?

6. What characteristics come to mind for someone with "poor character"?

7. In what types of situations is your character tested each day? How is the character of your children tested?

Answer question 7 with your spouse. After answering, you may want to share an appropriate insight or discovery with the group.

The Core of Character

We often think of *character* in terms of qualities such as honesty, courage, and patience. A simple way to define character is: *Character is the outward expression of what is inside a person.* The choices we make, the way we treat other people, and the way we respond to circumstances are all governed by what's inside.

For a discussion about what is inside a person, there is no better source for guidance than God's Word.

8. What do the following Scripture passages tell us about the source of character?

• Proverbs 1:1-7

• Galatians 5:22-23

• James 3:13-18

9. Read Psalm 78:1-8. What additional insight does this passage provide about

• the source of God-honoring character?

• the most important legacy we should leave our children?

10. Psalm 78:8 describes the results of not leaving a God-honoring legacy when it describes the *forefathers* as "a stubborn and rebellious generation, whose hearts were not loyal to God, whose spirits were not faithful to him." How is this like or unlike the conditions in our society today?

11. As parents we naturally want our children to get a good education and gain certain talents and skills. Sometimes we spend an enormous amount of time, money, and effort helping them learn and grow in these areas. What are practical ways we can also invest in their character development? What can happen to a child who receives inadequate character education?

HomeBuilders Principle:
The greatest legacy you can leave with your children is God-honoring character rooted in God and the Bible.

Great Traits

After completing the Wrap-Up activity, close this session in prayer. Before leaving, couples are encouraged to "Make a Date" to do this session's HomeBuilders Project.

As you focus on building character in your children, what character traits do you think are the most valuable for your children to learn and exhibit? As a group, brainstorm a top ten list of positive characteristics. Be sure to write down the final list, as it will be referred to in this session's HomeBuilders Project.

1.	6.
2.	7.
3.	8.
4.	9.
5.	10.

After the list has been compiled, discuss ways you could highlight or focus on the number one trait in your families this week.

Make a Date

Make a date with your spouse to complete the Home-Builders Project for this session. Your leader will ask at the next meeting for you to share one thing from this experience.

DATE

TIME

LOCATION

HOMEBUILDERS PROJECT · 6 0   M I N U T E S

As a Couple [10 minutes]

Start this project by discussing these questions:

* From what you know, in what ways are your parents like their parents? As your parents get older, would you say they are becoming more or less like their parents? Explain.

If the group did not complete the Wrap-Up (page 20) during the session, finish that exercise with your spouse in place of discussing the "As a Couple" questions here.

- As you get older, would you say you are becoming more or less like your parents? Explain.

- Based on your observations about yourselves and your parents, what do you feel is the likely trend for your children?

Individually [20 minutes]

1. Look back through the questions you discussed during the group discussion. What is one thing you learned?

2. What type of legacy do you think you have received from your own parents? Write down at least three to five ways their lives influenced you. (Even if you didn't grow up with one of your parents, you may still be able to analyze the type of legacy he or she gave you—good or bad. Also, depending on your own family background, for this question you may want to focus on a person who helped raise you or had a profound influence on you rather than on your parents.)

3. How do you want your children to remember you? Try to summarize this in one sentence.

4. Read Psalm 78:1-8. What do you learn in this passage about
• how you should raise your children?

• what type of legacy you should leave them?

5. Look back at the top ten list the group created (page 20). For each of your children, what is one trait you would say is a strength and one that is a weakness? What about for yourself? Which trait does your spouse do a particularly good job of modeling to your children?

6. Thinking back over the last week, how would you rate yourself on a scale of 1 (low) to 10 (high) on being intentional about developing character in your children? Explain.

Interact as a Couple [30 minutes]

1. Share your answers from the individual section. As you discuss your responses, be open, kind, and understanding. Make an effort to listen without interrupting.

2. Think about the time, effort, and money you have given to developing your children. Based on what you have invested in, what would you say your priorities have been? How well would you say you've emphasized their character development to this point?

3. Discuss the primary goals you have for your children. Write these down as well as one step you agree to initiate this week to help build character in your children.

4. Close by each of you completing the following sentence: "My prayer for our children's character is..."

Be sure to check out the related Parent-Child Interaction on page 93.

The Foundation for Character

The key components that establish the foundation of God-honoring character are a relationship with Christ and obedience to God's Word.

W A R M • U P   15   M I N U T E S

Peer Pressure

Choose one of the following questions to answer and share with the group:

- As a child or teenager, when was a time you remember giving in to the pressure of friends and peers and making a poor choice?

- When is a time you made a right choice despite pressure and temptation to choose otherwise?

- When is a time recently that your child faced peer pressure? What happened? (Don't share anything that would violate the trust of your child.)

Project Report

Share one thing you learned from last session's HomeBuilders Project.

BLUEPRINTS   **6 0   M I N U T E S**

As we discussed in Session One, character is the outward expression of what's inside a person. To make the right choices in today's world, what is *inside* you needs to be stronger than the pressures and temptations *outside*. In this session we'll talk about what we need to teach our children about the foundation for a strong inner character.

All Your Heart, Soul, and Mind

The first component in the foundation for strong character is a growing relationship with Jesus.

Case Study

Until his senior year of high school, Alex was the one everyone admired. He was hard-working, energetic, enthusiastic, and dependable. Other students enjoyed being with him. He grew up in a church-going family and was involved in his church youth group. He knew the Bible well (in fact, he had often won Bible memory contests) and avoided temptations that seemed to trip up other kids.

If you have a large group, form smaller groups of about six people to answer the Blueprints questions. Unless otherwise noted, answer the questions in your subgroup. Before moving on to the Wrap-Up section, have sub-groups report to the whole group the highlights from their discussions.

When he returned for his final year in high school, something was different about Alex. He looked just as handsome and clean-cut on the outside, but his behavior changed. He began frequenting the parties he once avoided, and it was not unusual for him to drive home drunk or stoned. He seemed determined to try all the things he had previously denied himself, and he took risks in how he drove and how he treated other people. When a friend asked him one Sunday why he wasn't in church, he replied, "I don't do that anymore. I got tired of hearing people tell me all the things I couldn't do."

1. What do you suspect is behind the changes in Alex?

2. As a teenager, what was your attitude toward God? What effect did this have on your behavior?

3. What can we do as parents to try and keep our children from heading down the path Alex chose?

4. What do the following passages tell us about the type of commitment God calls for us to make to him? How would you paraphrase these verses to make them understandable to your children?

• Matthew 22:36-38

• Romans 12:1-2

• Galatians 2:20

HomeBuilders Principle:
God-honoring character should be a reflection of an ongoing relationship with Christ.

A Lamp Unto Our Feet

In John 14:15, Jesus says, "If you love me, you will obey what I command." This points to a second component in the foundation for strong character—a commitment to knowing and obeying God's Word.

5. Read Psalm 119:97-106. What does this passage tell us about the practical benefits of following the precepts of God's Word?

6. What does the verse, "Your word is a lamp to my feet and a light for my path" (Psalm 119:105) mean? What are some ways God's Word has been a light to your path?

7. In our culture today we increasingly hear that there is no objective, eternal truth—that each person can determine his or her own truth. If a child grows up with the belief that truth is subjective, what type of character do you think will emerge?

8. Read Psalm 1. What promises are given to those who delight in God's Word?

HomeBuilders Principle:
God-honoring character requires an inner commitment to obeying God's Word, no matter what.

Building the Foundation

It's one thing to realize that we, as parents, need a committed relationship with Christ and a commitment to obeying God's Word. But how do we help our children establish that foundation for God-honoring character? Here are a couple suggestions:

Answer questions 9 and 10 with your spouse. After answering, you may want to share an appropriate insight or discovery with the group.

Show your children the attractiveness of a love relationship with Christ not only through teaching but also by example.

9. In what ways can you *show* your children how to walk closely with God?

10. Why do you think they need to see this relationship modeled in your life?

Take advantage of everyday moments to show your children how to apply God's Word to their lives.

11. What does Deuteronomy 6:6-7 tell us about how we should teach God's Word to our children?

12. With your spouse, choose one of the following scenarios. Discuss how the situation you selected could be turned into a teachable moment to help a child learn about applying God's Word to his or her life. Then share your insights with the group.
* A child is watching a television show that you find questionable.

* One child has taken another's toy, and in return received a fist in the stomach.

- A teenager is given a stolen copy of an upcoming geometry test.

W R A P • U P   15   M I N U T E S

Telling Stories

After completing the Wrap-Up activity, close this session in prayer. Before leaving, couples are encouraged to "Make a Date" to do this session's Home-Builders Project.

One practical way to reach your children is by taking advantage of their natural love for stories by telling them stories about your experiences as a Christian. This will encourage them in their relationship with Christ.

Select one of the following topics for which to share a brief story with the group (and later with your children!):

- how you began a relationship with Christ
- one or two milestones of your Christian experience
- a time when you clearly saw how God's Word could help you deal with a difficult situation
- a trial or time of suffering when God gave you strength and courage

- something you've learned lately from Scripture
- changes you've seen God make in your life

Make a Date

Make a date with your spouse to complete this session's HomeBuilders Project. Your leader will ask at the next meeting for you to share one thing from this experience.

DATE

TIME

LOCATION

HOMEBUILDERS PROJECT · 60 MINUTES

As a Couple [10 minutes]

Start this date by talking about one of your favorite fictional characters from books, the movies, or television from when you were a child or a teenager.

- What traits did you admire in this character and why?

- In what ways, if any, did this character influence how you acted?
- As an adult and a parent do you still like this character? Why or why not?

Individually [20 minutes]

1. What is one way you were challenged by this session?

2. Ranking yourself on a scale of 1 (low) to 10 (high), how well do you feel you have modeled the attractiveness of a love relationship with Christ to your children? Explain. (If you have questions about your relationship with Christ, we encourage you to read the article "Our Problems, God's Answers" starting on page 108.)

3. Ranking yourself on a scale of 1 (low) to 10 (high), how well do you think you have modeled the importance of obeying God's Word? Explain.

4. In the session Wrap-Up, we talked about the importance of telling stories to your children to encourage them in their relationship with Christ. For each box in the following grid, write down some thoughts of what you would like to share with your family.

How I began a relationship with Christ	How God's Word has helped me deal with difficult situations
Milestones of my Christian walk	Times of trial or suffering when God's Word gave me strength and courage
Changes I've seen God make in my life	Something I've been learning from Scripture

Interact as a Couple [30 minutes]

1. Share what you wrote down during your individual time.

2. Make plans for when you will begin telling your faith stories to your children.

_____
DATE

_____
TIME

_____
PLACE

3. For each of your children, discuss how you see them and what you can do to encourage them in relation to the foundational character building components of
• a relationship with Christ.
• obedience to God's Word.

4. Pray for God's help and wisdom as you model for your children a relationship with Christ and obedience to God's Word.

Be sure to check out the related Parent-Child Interaction on page 95.

Your Family's Character

You can encourage God-honoring character in your children by establishing it in the environment of your home.

W A R M • U P   15   M I N U T E S

Famous Families

When you think of the following real and fictional families, what words come to mind? What kind of reputation do these families have? What qualities characterize them?

- The Kennedys
- The Huxtables ("The Cosby Show")
- King David's family
- The Barones ("Everybody Loves Raymond")
- The Windsors (Britain's royal family)
- "The Addams Family"

(continued on next page)

- The Husseins (former ruling family in Iraq)
- "The Waltons"
- The Grahams (Billy, Ruth and family)
- The Cleavers ("Leave It to Beaver")

Project Report

Share one thing you learned from last session's HomeBuilders Project.

BLUEPRINTS   60 MINUTES

What's Your Reputation?

If you have a large group, form smaller groups of about six people to answer the Blueprints questions. Unless otherwise noted, answer the questions in your subgroup. Before moving on to the Wrap-Up section, have sub-groups report to the whole group the highlights from their discussions.

Every group of people develops a character of its own, based on what the group does, how it behaves, and how it treats people. Companies and corporations, restaurants and local stores, schools and athletic teams, churches and ministries—all build a reputation based on their character. This character is established in large part by each group's leadership, and it influences the behavior of every person in the group.

1. What is an example of a local store, business, or restaurant that has built a good reputation in your community? How would you characterize this institution?

2. When the apostle Paul wrote his letters to different churches, he often began by speaking of their reputation. What does Paul say about the reputation of the churches in the following passages?
* Colossians 1:3-8

* 1 Thessalonians 1:2-10

3. Families also develop their own character. They may develop a reputation for being generous, snobbish, hospitable, strange, fun, creative, messy,

---

interesting, and so on. What is one family you know or have known with definite character? Briefly describe this family to the group.

4. How do you think other people viewed your family as you grew up? What was your family's reputation?

5. Read Joshua 24:14-15. What challenge do these verses offer to us as parents? How do you think our families should be different from those that do not seek to serve the Lord?

Your Family's Environment

Your family's character is shaped by many things, some of which you can't control. Things like your family background, where you live, your individual personalities, and your financial status, to name a few. One key factor that you can control is the environment in your family. This involves making choices about the things you do and the way you relate to each other. One of the best ways to develop Christ-like character within your children is by weaving God-honoring character into the environment of your home.

6. What are some things you wish you did more often as a family? What's keeping you from doing those things?

Answer questions 6 and 7 with your spouse. After answering, you may want to share an appropriate insight or discovery with the group.

7. The Scriptures contain many passages about how to treat others, and these have direct application within the family. For each of the following passages, what is one way you could apply this counsel better in your home?

• Colossians 3:13

• 1 Peter 3:8-10

Your Family's Values

Another key to establishing your family's character is deciding what you believe in—what values provide the foundation of your home. Much of who I (Crawford) am today was forged because I grew up in a family characterized by biblical values that were passed on from generation to generation. My great-grandfather, Peter, was a former slave who was committed to his family and also had a great heart for God—he was known for singing and praying on his front porch and for the Scripture passages he memorized by having family members recite them over and over.

My grandfather, Milton, also had a God-honoring walk. He was committed to the church and was superintendent of the Sunday school. The Word of God and prayer were clear priorities in his household. He passed these values onto his fourteen children, including my father, who was the greatest man I've ever known. Pop was quiet about his faith, but it formed the core of his character and of our home. He worked hard to provide for his family and was committed to helping people in need—relatives, neighbors, and friends in church.

I don't think a week goes by that I don't think about my great-grandfather, Peter. I never met him, but I know what he gave us—a core, a foundation for our family's character. From my family history I can discern two different steps for establishing this character: Decide what you're going to stand for, and develop creative ways to emphasize these values.

8. What positive values and character qualities did your parents pass down to you? How well do you think you're doing in passing these on to your children?

9. Review the "Loritts Family Values" (p. 46). What are expressions similar to these that you've heard—either in your family or in other families?

Loritts Family Values

A Loritts tradition has been to summarize some of our most important values in expressions that are passed on from generation to generation. For example, the exhortations, "You never walk away from responsibility" and "You take care of your family first" speak to our commitment to the family. When we repeat them often enough, our children remember them.

It's important to put your highest priority on values based not on personal preferences but on Scripture. Some couples, for example, have a list of "favorite" Scriptures they teach their children. One of the best ways to discern eternal biblical values is to look for passages that provide broad exhortations about what is most important in life.

1. You never walk away from responsibility (Colossians 3:23-24).
2. You take care of your family first (1 Timothy 5:8).
3. Don't ever tell God how to use you (Acts 20:24; Romans 12:1-2).
4. What God has for you, no one can take away from you (2 Timothy 4:7-8; 1 Corinthians 15:58).
5. Don't live by your rights, but respond to what is right (Galatians 2:20).
6. Don't operate from giftedness but from brokenness (Psalm 51:16-17).
7. God created you to make a difference (Acts 20:24; 1 Peter 2:9-10).
8. Life is all about God (Ephesians 3:20-21).
9. Your character will feed your conduct no matter what the circumstances (Daniel 1:8).

10. With each couple taking one or more of the following passages, read your verses with your spouse, and discuss what Scripture is urging us to do and what values you find. Then report to the group a summary of your verses and insights.

- Philippians 1:6-11
- Philippians 2:21-27
- Colossians 1:9-12
- Colossians 3:1-4

- Colossians 3:5-11
- Colossians 3:12-14
- Colossians 3:15-17
- 1 Peter 4:10-11

11. Who is a family you know that has a reputation for God-honoring character? Describe this family, and tell what you know about how the parents emphasize biblical values with their children.

W R A P • U P   15   M I N U T E S

A Good Name

One of the most important questions you can ask yourself as a parent is, "What do I want my family to be known for?" You will explore this question in

---

greater depth during the HomeBuilders Project. However, starting now, with your spouse take a few minutes to discuss and write down a short list of values you agree that you want your family to exemplify. Then pick one or two of the things you wrote down to share with the group.

Make a Date

Make a date with your spouse to complete the HomeBuilders Project for this session.

_____
DATE

_____
TIME

_____
LOCATION

Parting Thought

For some of you, this may be the first time you've seriously thought about your family's character. As you look at the environment in your home and the reputation of your family, you may wonder if it's too late to make any changes. Let us assure you that it is never too late! God delights in reviving a family just as he does a wayward soul.

A good first step is to complete this session's Home-Builders Project, which will help you develop a plan for establishing your family's character. Spend a few weeks emphasizing these character qualities individually and as a couple, and then call a family meeting to talk about what you want to see happen in your family. Don't be afraid to confess any failure on your part. Tell your children specifically what you want your family to be known for and what you're going to emphasize as parents.

HOMEBUILDERS PROJECT　　　6 0　　M I N U T E S

As a Couple [10 minutes]

There are many creative ways to emphasize certain values as you build your family's character. One practical way to do this is to develop a family mission statement. Together, create a one or two sentence draft of a mission statement. Then after you have

---

completed the rest of this HomeBuilders Project, come back to the statement you wrote to see if there are any changes you would like to make to it. Consider this a work in progress. You may want to revisit and polish this statement throughout the duration of this course. Once you have a final version, you might want to display it in your home or print it onto cards for each member of your family to have.

Individually [20 minutes]

1. What's one insight or concept from this session that you want to apply in your life or in the life of your family?

2. Being as objective as you can, how would you describe the character of your family at this time?

3. How do you think other people view your family?

4. What type of environment do you want to have in your home? Respond to the questions that follow to spur your thinking.

- What things do you want to do together as a family?

- How do you want to spend your evenings?

- How do you want to spend your weekends?

- What type of vacations do you want to plan?

- What atmosphere do you want to establish during dinners together?

- What are you doing too much of as a family?

- What are you not doing enough of as a family?

- How are we treating each other?

- How should we be treating each other?

- What can we do as parents to teach our children how to properly relate to each other?

Interact as a Couple [30 minutes]

1. Share your answers from the individual time.

2. Make a list of six to eight character qualities or values you want for your family. Try and include a related Scripture reference for each. Then discuss which items on your list you feel are the most important and how you can emphasize these in your home.

3. Write down how you would like your children to complete this sentence in twenty years: "As I was growing up, my family was…"

4. Pray for God to help you live out and pass down the values you have identified.

Be sure to check out the related Parent-Child Interaction on page 97.

The Enemy of Character

Our natural foolishness hinders any effort to build God-honoring character.

W A R M • U P   15   M I N U T E S

Do the Right Thing

Pick one of the following four scenarios and share with the group what you would do. Share what you think would be a wise response and what would be a foolish response in this situation and why.

- Your doctor has told you that you have developed an extremely unusual condition. Due to a genetic abnormality, you can eat anything you want without gaining more weight.

- You are walking alone through a wooded park and find a large satchel stuffed with unmarked

$100 bills. You look around, and you can't see or hear anyone.

- You're supposed to go to your small group tonight, but you had an exhausting day at work, and you just noticed there's a movie you've been wanting to see on TV tonight.
- You just made plans for a night out with friends when your in-laws call to announce a surprise visit for the same day and time.

After everyone has shared their answers, discuss this question: Even when the wise choice is clear, why isn't it always easy to make the right decision?

Project Report

Share one thing you learned from last session's HomeBuilders Project.

BLUEPRINTS   60 MINUTES

Wise and Foolish

Within each of us lies a hidden enemy of God-honoring character. This enemy is our sin nature that leads us to seek our own pleasure and our own desires. This is the heart described in Isaiah 53:6 "We all, like sheep, have gone astray, each of us has turned to his own way."

1. With each couple taking one or more of the following passages, discuss what your verses say about the characteristics of the wise and of the foolish. Then report your findings to the group.

If you have a large group, form smaller groups of about six people to answer the Blueprints questions. Unless otherwise noted, answer the questions in your subgroup. Before moving on to the Wrap-Up section, have sub-groups report to the whole group the highlights from their discussions.

- Psalm 36:1-4
- Proverbs 1:1-7
- Proverbs 8:32-36
- Proverbs 10:9-11
- Proverbs 12:15-16
- Proverbs 14:15-16

2. Proverbs 22:15 tells us "folly is bound up in the heart of a child." What makes the foolishness of children different from the foolishness of adults? How do children typically display foolishness?

3. What are some foolish choices your children have made lately?

Answer question 3 with your spouse. After answering, you may want to share an appropriate insight or discovery with the group. (Remember, don't share anything that would violate the trust of your children.)

4. Why do you think some people never seem to stop making foolish choices about their lives?

5. What has to happen to get people to stop making foolish choices?

Driving Foolishness Away

Whenever I (Crawford) did something downright foolish, my Pop would give me a penetrating look and say, "So you want to act the monkey." It was his way of saying, "Boy, you have better sense than that." He knew that it was a dangerous thing to allow a child's foolishness to go unchecked.

To address this issue in your children, we have three suggestions:

- Give your children practice in saying no to foolish impulses and yes to the right things in life.
- Allow your children to experience the consequences of foolishness.
- Provide your children with accountability for their actions.

Saying No to Foolish Impulses and Yes to the Right Things

Training children in making wise decisions involves monitoring the behavior of your children and continually calling them to right choices.

6. One area where children need training is in *how they talk to others*. When your children follow their impulses, how do they talk to one another or to their friends?

7. What do the following verses tell us about the tongue of the wise and the tongue of the foolish?

• Proverbs 10:18-20

• Proverbs 12:17-19

• Proverbs 15:1-2

8. If a child continually says mean and hurtful things to a sibling, how could you step in and help him or her say no to foolish impulses?

9. How can gaining practice in saying no to foolish impulses benefit your children as they grow into adults? If children don't receive this training, what problems do you predict they will face—especially as teenagers and young adults?

Experiencing the Consequences of Foolishness

The wise parent will use consequences as a learning tool and as a form of discipline. This is especially useful for children between ten and twenty. Sometimes experience is the only school a fool will attend.

10. How could you use consequences to teach
- a preteen child what happens when bad choices about money are made?

- a new driver the cost of poor driving choices?

Providing Accountability

Parenting provides a natural opportunity for accountability because children learn that someone will call them to account for their behavior.

11. Read Proverbs 12:15; 14:12; and 28:26. Why do fools want to avoid accountability for their choices? What benefits are there in allowing yourself to be held accountable by others?

12. There are a number of ways to provide accountability. Consider as an example that one of your children is stealing cookies from the pantry. What could you do to help hold this child accountable through

For question 12, each couple should focus on answering one of the bullet point questions. Then share your response with the group.

- rewarding for good choices and disciplining for poor choices?

- helping the child understand why he or she is making poor choices?

- using this incident to help the child see his or her need for God?

HomeBuilders Principle:
Foolishness cannot be allowed to go unchecked in a child.

W R A P • U P   15 M I N U T E S

Just Say No!

What are common circumstances our children regularly face where help and training to say no to foolish impulses is needed? As a group, come up with a list.

In general, which items do you feel present the biggest challenge to your children? For the top one or two things identified, discuss practical ways you can train your children to say no in the face of these circumstances.

Make a Date

Make a date with your spouse to complete this session's HomeBuilders Project.

DATE

TIME

LOCATION

HOMEBUILDERS PROJECT   6 0   M I N U T E S

As a Couple [10 minutes]

As parents, sometimes we get so focused on watching our kids—looking out for the wrong things they do—that we can forget the importance of catching them doing good things. When is a time you "caught" your children doing the right thing—making a wise decision that made you proud? When is a time your spouse has made you proud?

Individually [20 minutes]

1. Looking back through this session, what point is most relevant to your family right now and why?

2. What were some of the foolish things you did when you were a child? a teenager?

3. How would you describe a person who is a fool?

4. When is a time in your life when you could have been described as a fool? What helped you turn away from foolishness?

5. In what areas of your life are you most tempted to make foolish choices now?

6. What are examples of both wise and foolish choices you've seen each of your children make lately?

7. How could you improve in providing account-ability for the choices your children make and in helping them to learn how to say no to foolish impulses?

Interact as a Couple [30 minutes]

1. Share your answers from the individual time.

2. Using your answers from question 6 from the individual section, fill out the following chart for your children. (If you need additional space, you have permission to photocopy this chart, or you can re-create this yourself on a separate piece of paper.)

Child's Name	Wise Choices	Foolish Choices

3. Write down one or two things you can do to address foolishness in each of your children.

4. Close in prayer.

Be sure to check out the related Parent-Child Interaction on page 99.

Keeping Our Character

Character is built during times of testing.

For Extra Impact: Do this Warm-Up in complete darkness. **Leader:** See Leader Note number 1 on page 136.

Let There Be Light!

Discuss these questions:

- When was a time you found yourself in a dark place, unable to see, and without a candle or flashlight available? What happened? What did it feel like?

- What do you think it would be like to live for a month in that condition—in total darkness, without any light?

- How would you compare the experience of coping in the darkness to the spiritual condition of a person who does not know Christ?

Project Report

Share one thing you learned from last session's HomeBuilders Project.

BLUEPRINTS   60 MINUTES

We never enjoy times of testing and trial, but they are an integral part of our growth in Christ. An untested faith is a weak and uncertain faith. Character is formed in the crucible of testing and suffering.

Living in the Darkness

If you have a large group, form smaller groups of about six people to answer the Blueprints questions. Unless otherwise noted, answer the questions in your subgroup. Before moving on to the Wrap-Up section, have subgroups report to the whole group the highlights from their discussions.

The Scriptures often use the metaphor of light and darkness to illustrate critical truths. Those who do not know Christ, for example, are said to "walk in darkness" (John 8:12). But light always overcomes darkness—never the other way around.

1. In what ways does our culture make it difficult for us to trust and obey God? What is an example of how your faith has been tested by the world?

2. What are ways you see your children being tested by the darkness of our world?

3. Read John 1:9-10 and John 8:12. What do you think it means that Jesus is "the light of the world"?

4. Psalm 119:105 tells us God's Word "is a lamp to my feet and a light for my path." How have you seen God's Word provide light for you or your children in the midst of darkness?

5. Read Matthew 5:14-16 and Ephesians 5:8-11. What do you think it means to "let your light shine before men" and to "live as children of light"? Practically, what are examples of how we—including our children—can do this?

6. The Bible also warns us to keep ourselves from being polluted by the world (James 4:4) and to not be conformed to the pattern of this world (Romans 12:2). How can a Christian be a light in the world without becoming polluted by it?

7. As parents, we desire to protect our children from the darkness of the world. Yet we also need to train and encourage them to be a light in the darkness. How can we accomplish both?

HomeBuilders Principle:
The Christian life is to be lived in the midst of darkness, and our children must learn to be lights for Christ.

Living Through Trials

8. Read James 1:2-5. How is our faith tested during trials?

9. When is a time your faith was tested by some type of trial? What happened? How was your relationship with God affected?

10. How strong do you think a person's relationship with God would be if he or she never faced any trials or problems in life? Explain.

11. Read Psalm 27:7-14. What do we learn in this passage about what we need to do to maintain our dependence on God during trials?

12. What specific problems or trials do you foresee your children facing during the next few years? What can you begin or continue doing to help prepare them to cope with these situations?

Answer question 12 with your spouse. After answering, you may want to share an appropriate insight or discovery with the group.

Case Studies

Following are some typical situations in which the character of your children might be tested. With your spouse, select one to discuss. Read your scenario, and answer the discussion questions at the end. Then share your answers with the group.

Scenario 1

Your twelve-year-old son is listening to his favorite radio station, and you overhear a song with violent and obscene lyrics.

Scenario 2

The company where you work is in a slump and was forced to reduce your salary by 20 percent. This will lead to a severe cutback in your family budget—you've got to reduce your entertainment and clothing budgets, you won't be able to buy a new car as you'd hoped, and you won't be taking your family out of town on vacation this year. You've even wondered if you need to sell your home and move into a smaller one that is less expensive.

Scenario 3

Your sixteen-year-old daughter is a cheerleader and is not comfortable with the lewd and suggestive dancing that the squad is being taught. When she talks with the cheerleading instructor, the routines are changed, but some of the other cheerleaders are upset and say she is judgmental and has a "holier than thou" attitude.

Discussion questions:

- What choices do you think need to be made?

- What, if any, Scripture passages you can think of applies to this situation and can be taken into consideration?

- What would you tell your child in this situation? For what does he or she need to trust God?

Make a Date

Make a date with your spouse to complete this session's HomeBuilders Project.

DATE

TIME

LOCATION

HOMEBUILDERS PROJECT   6 0   M I N U T E S

As a Couple [10 minutes]

To start this project, take turns telling each other about a character building experience you had growing up that taught you a valuable lesson. Use these questions to help guide your discussion:

- What happened?
- What lesson did you learn?
- How has this experience shaped and influenced your character?

Individually [20 minutes]

1. What is something new—good or bad—that this session revealed to you?

2. In what ways do you think God has used you to be a "light" in darkness?

3. In what ways has he used your spouse to be a light? your children?

4. What has been the most severe test of your character and of your faith?

5. What do you appreciate about how your spouse responds to testing and trials? What do you think could be improved in the way you typically respond to testing and trials?

6. What could be improved in how your children generally respond to the trials in their lives?

7. What are two or three things you want your children to learn about how they should respond to testing and trials?

Interact as a Couple [30 minutes]

1. Share your answers from the individual time.

2. Talk about any trials or tests your children are facing right now.
• How can you help them?

• In what ways do they need to trust God?

3. Write down two or three action points that you can implement as a couple to help your children build their character during times of testing and trial.

4. Pray specifically for each of your children and any trials they are currently facing.

Be sure to check out the related Parent-Child Interaction on page 101.

Modeling Character

You are the primary example your children have for what kinds of people they should become.

W A R M • U P   15   M I N U T E S

A Chip off the Block

Complete one of the following sentences, and then share it with the group.

- "I am just like my (pick one) mother/father in that I…"

- "One thing I learned from my mother/father that I'll never forget is…"

- "One way my son/daughter is just like me is…"

Project Report

Share one thing you learned from last session's HomeBuilders Project.

BLUEPRINTS   60 MINUTES

Sharing Your Lives

1. Read 1 Thessalonians 2:7-12. How does the Apostle Paul describe his behavior when he ministered to the Thessalonians? What kind of model did he set for them?

If you have a large group, form smaller groups of about six people to answer the Blueprints questions. Unless otherwise noted, answer the questions in your subgroup. Before moving on to the Wrap-Up section, have sub-groups report to the whole group the highlights from their discussions.

2. What do you think Paul means when he says, "we were delighted to share with you not only the gospel of God but our lives as well"?

3. In this study we've defined character as "the outward expression of what is inside a person." Which do you think is more important as you build character in your children—what you say to them or how you live in front of them? Why?

4. What are some positive character qualities your parents modeled for you?

HomeBuilders Principle:
For good or bad, your character will shape that of your children.

Modeling Biblical Character

A list of all the qualities we should model to our children would be so long that we'd end up feeling discouraged and depressed over our inadequacy! Here are just a few we consider important.

Keeping Your Word

5. Read James 5:12. Why is it important for parents to follow through on promises to children?

Repentance and Forgiveness

6. Read Ephesians 4:32 and James 5:16. Why is it important for parents to both extend forgiveness to and seek forgiveness from their children?

7. Why is it often difficult for parents to ask forgiveness from their children? When is a time you asked forgiveness from your child or children and what was the result?

Trusting God

8. Read Psalm 37:3-5, and discuss the following action points from the passage. What is something you could do in the next week to model this to your children?

Answer question 8 with your spouse. After answering, you may want to share an appropriate insight or discovery with the group.

• "Trust in the Lord and do good."

• "Delight yourself in the Lord."

• "Commit your way to the Lord."

9. In the book of 1 Timothy, Paul provides advice to Timothy for his ministry. Read 1 Timothy 4:7-12. How can we apply these verses to our responsibilities as parents?

10. 1 Timothy 4:12 instructs us to "set an example for the believers in speech, in life, in love, in faith and in purity." With each couple taking at least one of the topics called out in this verse, discuss this question: What are practical ways you can set an example for your children in this area? Be specific. After a few minutes, take turns reporting your ideas to the group.

• Speech

• Life

• Love

• Faith

• Purity

What's Next?

As you come to the end of this course, take a few
minutes to reflect on this experience. Review the
following questions, and write down responses to the
questions you can answer. Then relate to the group
one or more of your answers.

- What has this group meant to you over the
  course of this study? Be specific.

- What is the most valuable thing you have
  learned or discovered?

- How have you as a parent been changed or
  challenged?

- What would you like to see happen next for this group?

Make a Date

Make a date with your spouse to meet in the next week to complete the final HomeBuilders Project of this study.

DATE

TIME

LOCATION

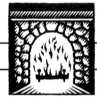

HOMEBUILDERS PROJECT · 6 0 M I N U T E S

As a Couple [10 minutes]

Congratulations—you've made it to the last project in this study! Start your date by reflecting on what impact this course has had on you by discussing these questions:

- What has been the best part of this study for you?
- How has this study benefited your marriage?
- In what ways has this course helped you as a parent?
- What is something new you learned or discovered about yourself? your spouse? your children?

Individually [20 minutes]

1. What point from this session had the most impact on you and why?

2. Overall, what has been the most important insight or lesson for you from this course?

3. What is one character strength and one character weakness you believe you inherited from your father or mother?

4. What are character qualities you believe you model well for your children?

5. What are qualities your spouse models well?

6. Galatians 5:22-23 says, "But the fruit of the Spirit is love, joy, peace, patience, kindness, goodness, faithfulness, gentleness and self-control."

- What is a situation you faced recently where you had the opportunity to model an aspect of the fruit of the Spirit to your children? What aspect or aspects did you model well? Which aspects do you wish you had modeled better?

- What is a specific situation you are currently facing where you have an opportunity to model the aspects of the fruit of the Spirit to your children? Pray for God's help to set a God-honoring example as you deal with this situation.

7. How would you complete the sentence that follows?

"If I don't change _____,
my children are likely to be just like me in that area.
Pray for God's help in setting a good example in
the area you identified.

Interact as a Couple [30 minutes]

1. Share your answers from the individual section.

2. Identify a step or action—something you want
to do, stop doing, or change—that you noted during
this course and that you need to follow through
on. What needs to happen for this to become a
reality?

3. Evaluate what you should do or continue to do
to strengthen your family. You may want to consider

continuing the practice of setting aside time for date nights. Review the list of ideas on page 107.

4. Spend a few minutes praying together. Thank God for each other and for your children. Pray for God's wisdom, direction, and blessing as you continue to build character in your children.

Be sure to check out the related Parent-Child Interaction on page 102.

Please visit our Web site at www. familylife.com/homebuilders to give us your feedback on this study and to get information on other FamilyLife resources and conferences.

Parent-Child Interactions

The object of each of these Parent-Child Interactions is to help parents connect with their children and to help build their character. Make these a special occasion. Consider doing these as part of a weekly or monthly family night.

Interaction 1

What Kind of Person Are You?

1. Instruct your children to each write down the names of five people they know from outside your family. These could be friends, teachers, anybody. Then tell them to write down one or two words that describe each of the people on their list. Is this person kind? cruel? selfish? giving?

Supply your children with paper and something to write with for this interaction.

2. Have each person in your family share what he or she wrote down. Ask each child to give an example of how he or she observed a certain quality in another person. (If negative things are shared about someone, you may want to use this as an opportunity to talk about what is appropriate and what is not to talk about outside of this family gathering.)

3. Say: **You may not realize it, but you were describing different parts of the *character* of each person on your list. Character is the outward expression of what is inside a person. If a person is selfish on the inside, he or she will show it on the outside in how that person treats other people. What we often don't**

---

realize is how our character influences other people. The way we act can influence other people to act the same.

4. Tell your children an example of someone you've observed (at work, at school, at home, in public) who had a specific, positive influence because of his or her character. Then tell them about someone who had a negative influence because of his or her character.

5. Tell your children to look again at their lists. Ask: **When one of these people is kind or loving or generous, how does that make you feel? How does that make you want to act with this person?**

6. Say: **As your parents, we want to have a positive influence on you. We call this our "legacy"—we want you to know the type of people we are, and what we think is important. We want you to grow up with the knowledge that we've passed something significant on to you. Chances are, the lessons we teach you will last longer in your minds than the lessons from almost anyone else.**

7. Ask a child to read aloud Proverbs 1:8-9.

Ask: **Why do you think this passage tells children to listen to the instruction of their parents?**

8. Have a volunteer read aloud Psalm 78:1-8. Then ask:

- **In this passage, what are parents told to tell their children?**
- **Why do you think it's important for us, as your parents, to tell you to put your trust in God, to not forget his deeds, and to keep his commands?**

9. Close your time in prayer, using Psalm 78:1-8 as a guide. Ask God to build your family so that you put your trust in him, not forget his deeds, and keep his commands.

Interaction 2

Remembering

The foundation for God-honoring character is a relationship with Christ. One of the best ways to encourage your children to walk with Christ is to tell them stories about your own experiences as a Christian. Before scheduling this interaction, be sure to complete the HomeBuilders Project for Session Two (starting on page 35). In this project you are asked to write down things you can share with your family in several different areas. For this interaction you will tell your children about how you began a relationship with Christ.

This interaction introduces the concept of a Legacy Box. Find a box or container that can become your family's Legacy Box. You may want to decorate or label this ahead of time or, depending on the ages of your children, incorporate this as a family event.

You will receive instructions and ideas for various papers and objects to place in your Legacy Box, starting with this interaction and continuing through the remaining interactions. Each item that goes into the box will signify part of the legacy you will leave your children.

To help you tell your story about how you began a relationship with Christ, make a photocopy of your official birth certificate, and then decide on something that signifies your "rebirth." This might be an old photo, a baptism certificate, an old Bible or other significant book—anything that represents to you how God worked in your life to bring you into a relationship with Christ.

1. Ask:

- **Why do we observe holidays such as Thanksgiving and the Fourth of July?**
- **Why do you think it's important for us to remember events like these?**

2. Read Psalm 78:1-8. Then say: **In the last interaction we talked about this passage, which instructs us to always remember the things God does for us. An example of people who remembered God can be found in the Bible in the book of Joshua. In Joshua, the people of God have left Egypt, where they were held in captivity, and are now trying to regain their old land.**

3. Have your children take turns reading parts of Joshua 3:5–4:7.

4. Ask: **What did the people do in order to remember what God had done by stopping the river so they could cross?**

5. Now it's time to introduce the Legacy Box. Say: **We can create our own ways of remembering what God has done for us. We're going to use this Legacy Box to pass something of ourselves on to you. The things we put in this box are going to signify important things to us and to our family. One thing we're going to do is tell you a story about what God has done in our lives, and as we do this we're going to put some things in this**

Legacy Box that signify what God has done.

6. Now proceed to tell your children about how you began a relationship with Christ, and as you do, place in the box the copy of your birth certificate and the object signifying your new life in Christ.

Interaction 3

What Is Your Reputation?

Before doing this interaction, be sure you have completed the HomeBuilders Project for Session Three (starting on page 49); most important is the list of character values and traits you desire for your family. You will need to have copies of this list to give to your children as well as one to deposit into your Legacy Box.

1. Say: **Each of us has some type of reputation. Based on our character—how we treat people, how we react in different situations—people view us in a certain way. They say things like, "Jonathan is one of the quietest kids I've ever seen" or "Rachel is always mean to other people."**

2. Ask: **Who is someone you know who has a reputation of being a bully to other people? Who is someone who has a reputation as being loving and kind?**

3. Say: **Families also develop their own character. They may develop a reputation for being generous,**

---

strange, fun, smart, or messy. Tell your children about a family you knew while growing up—or a family you know now—that had a certain reputation. (A word of caution may be in order if you choose to talk about a family your children know.)

4. Tell your children about the type of reputation your family had while you were growing up.

5. Choose a family your kids know well (and that has a positive reputation), and ask: **What type of reputation does this family have?**

6. Ask for a volunteer to read Joshua 24:14-15 aloud. Then ask:

- **What do you think it means for a family to serve the Lord?**
- **If we are to serve the Lord as a family, how should that affect the way we treat other people?**

7. Have your children read aloud Colossians 3:13 and 1 Peter 3:8-10. Ask:

- **What do these Scriptures tell us about how to treat others?**
- **How can we make these things part of our family's character?**

8. Hand to your children the list of values you and your spouse created (as part of the HomeBuilders Project for Session Three) that you would like to form your family's character. Explain as much about each value as you feel is appropriate. When you are finished, place a copy of the list in the Legacy Box.

Interaction 4

Seeking Wisdom From God's Word

For the Legacy Box portion of this interaction, write a letter to each of your children. Talk about some of the positive qualities you've seen in their lives, and also tell them about the Christ-like character you pray will develop within them as they grow up.

1. Say: **We're going to play the game, "What Would You Do?" I'm going to describe a situation, and then you tell me what you think you should do.**

2. Read each of the following scenarios to your children:

- **A doctor has told you you have an extremely unusual condition—you can eat all the sweets and sugar you want for the rest of your life, and you will never gain any weight, get any cavities, or get sick as a result. Would you do it?**

- **You are walking through a wooded park and find a large bag stuffed with $100 bills. You look around, and you can't see or hear anyone. What would you do?**

3. Say: **Situations like these help us see that we need wisdom from God—from the Bible—in order to make good choices in our lives. Within each of us lies a hidden enemy of God-honoring character. This enemy is our sin nature that leads us to seek our own pleasure and our own desires. This is the heart described in Isaiah 53:6: "We all, like sheep, have gone astray, each of us has turned to his own way."**

4. Have your children read each of the following Bible passages, and after each one ask: **What does this passage say about a wise person or a foolish person?**

- Proverbs 1:5-7
- Proverbs 14:15-16
- Psalm 1:1-3

5. Ask: **What are some foolish things kids do?**

6. Say: **As we've read, we receive wisdom from God when we study and obey God's Word. For example, the Bible has a lot to tell us about how we should talk to other people—what we should say and how we should say it.**

7. Read the verses aloud that follow and then ask: **What do the following verses tell us about how we should talk to people?**

- Psalm 34:13
- Proverbs 8:7-8
- Proverbs 29:20

After your children answer the question for each verse, include some comments of your own to illustrate how this Scripture passage can be obeyed in your family. Use some real-life examples from your marriage and from what you've observed in how your children talk to each other.

8. Read to your children the letters you wrote to them, and then place the letters in the Legacy Box. Depending on the nature of what you wrote, you may want to do this with all your children together, or plan for one-on-one time.

Interaction 5
Living in Darkness

For this interaction you need a candle and matches. (If you have younger children, you may want to substitute a flashlight in place of the candle.)

You'll also be given another opportunity to share stories of your experiences as a Christian. You may wish to reference the notes you made during the Session Two HomeBuilders Project (see the chart on page 37).

1. By candle, lead your children into a room with no lights, where it is impossible to see in the dark. Blow out the candle. Wait about thirty seconds, and ask: **How does it feel when you find yourself without any light in a room like this?**

2. Then ask: **What do you think it would be like to live for an entire day or week in this situation—in total darkness, without any light?**

3. Light the candle, and then switch on the light. Have a child read aloud John 1:9-10 and John 8:12. Ask: **What do you think it means that Jesus is "the light of the world"?**

4. Say: **Psalm 119:105 tells us that God's Word "is a lamp to my feet and a light for my path."** Ask: **How has God's Word been a light to you or to our family?**

5. Place your candle in the Legacy Box to signify your family's commitment to following the light of God's Word. Then tell your children some stories about times when God's Word has given you insight into how to handle difficult situations.

For Extra Impact: To set a different environment for the stories you share, turn down the lights, and tell your stories by candlelight.

6. If you have time, tell your children some additional stories about milestones from your walk with Christ—important times in your life when you saw God at work in your lives.

Interaction 6

Living Through Trials

For this final interaction, you will begin a prayer notebook to keep in your Legacy Box. Purchase a spiral notebook or journal, or create your own notebook, or let your children make a family prayer notebook.

1. Ask:

- **What are some of the best days you've ever had?**
- **What are some of the worst days you can remember?**

2. Say: **Sometimes we wish things would always go well in life—that we would always be happy, always have fun, always be satisfied with what we do, and always get to be with the people we love. But life is not like that. At times things don't go the way we wish— things are harder than we want, or we suffer because of sickness or injury, or we lose someone we love.**

3. Have someone read aloud James 1:2-5. Ask:

- What do you think this passage means when it says, "Consider it pure joy...whenever you face trials of many kinds"?
- Why is it good for us to go through hard or tough times?
- How do you think going through hard times helps make our faith in God grow stronger?

4. Say: **Although we wish we didn't have to go through hard times, they are actually good for us because they lead us to seek a closer relationship with God and to trust God more with our lives.**

5. Have your children read aloud Psalm 27. Stop every few verses and ask: **What do we learn here about how God helps us in hard times and when we are hurting?**

6. Tell your children about a hard time you have faced and how this trial affected your relationship with God.

7. Say: **One way we can strengthen our faith in God is to pray about the difficult situations we face in life. We're going to start a family prayer journal and keep it in our Legacy Box. We will keep track of prayer requests and then record how God answers these prayers.** Then ask each member of the family to come up with at least one prayer request to begin the notebook.

Where Do You Go From Here?

It is our prayer that you have benefited greatly from this study in the HomeBuilders Parenting Series. We hope that your marriage and home will continue to grow stronger as you both submit your lives to Jesus Christ and build according to his blueprints.

We also hope that you will begin reaching out to strengthen other marriages in your community and local church. Your church needs couples like you who are committed to building Christian marriages. A favorite World War II story illustrates this point very clearly.

The year was 1940. The French Army had just collapsed under Hitler's onslaught. The Dutch had folded, overwhelmed by the Nazi regime. The Belgians had surrendered. And the British Army was trapped on the coast of France in the channel port of Dunkirk.

Two hundred and twenty thousand of Britain's finest young men seemed doomed to die, turning the English Channel red with their blood. The Fuehrer's troops, only miles away in the hills of France, didn't realize how close to victory they actually were.

Any rescue seemed feeble and futile in the time remaining. A "thin" British Navy—"the professionals"—told King George VI that at best they could save 17,000 troops. The House of Commons was warned to prepare for "hard and heavy tidings."

Politicians were paralyzed. The king was powerless. And the Allies could only watch as spectators from a distance. Then as the doom of the British Army seemed imminent, a strange fleet appeared on the horizon of the English Channel—the wildest assortment of boats perhaps ever assembled in history. Trawlers, tugs, scows, fishing sloops, lifeboats, pleasure craft, smacks and coasters, sailboats, even the London fire-brigade flotilla. *Each ship was manned by civilian volunteers—English fathers sailing to rescue Britain's exhausted, bleeding sons.*

William Manchester writes in his epic book, *The Last Lion*, that even today what happened in 1940 in less than twenty-four hours seems like a miracle—not only were all of the British soldiers rescued, but 118,000 other Allied troops as well.

Today the Christian home is much like those troops at Dunkirk. Pressured, trapped, and demoralized, it needs help. Your help. The Christian community may be much like England—we stand waiting for politicians, professionals, even for our pastors to step in and save the family. But the problem is much larger than all of those combined can solve.

With the highest divorce rate of any nation on earth, we need an all-out effort by men and women who are determined to help rescue the exhausted and wounded casualties of today's families. We need an outreach effort by common couples with faith in an uncommon God.

May we challenge you to invest your lives in others? You have one of the greatest opportunities in history—to help save today's families. By starting a HomeBuilders group, you can join couples around the world who are building and rebuilding hundreds of thousands of homes with a new, solid foundation of a relationship with God.

Will You Join Us in "Touching Lives...Changing Families"?

The following are some practical ways you can make a difference in families today:

1. Gather a group of four to eight couples, and lead them through the six sessions of this HomeBuilders study, *Building Character in Your Children.* (Why not consider challenging others in your church or community to form additional HomeBuilders groups?)

2. Commit to continue building your marriage and home by doing another course in the HomeBuilders Parenting Series or by leading a study in the HomeBuilders Couples Series.

3. An excellent outreach tool is the film *JESUS*, which is available on video. For more information, contact FamilyLife at 1-800-FL-TODAY.

4. Host a dinner party. Invite families from your neighborhood to your home, and as a couple share your faith in Christ.

5. Reach out and share the love of Christ with neighborhood children.

6. If you have attended the Weekend to Remember conference, why not offer to assist your pastor in counseling couples engaged to be married, using the material you received?

For more information about any of the above ministry opportunities, contact your local church, or write:

FamilyLife
P.O. Box 8220
Little Rock, AR 72221-8220
1-800-FL-TODAY
www.familylife.com

Our Problems, God's Answers

Every couple eventually has to deal with problems in marriage. Communication problems. Parenting issues. Money problems. Difficulties with sexual intimacy. These issues are important to cultivating a strong, loving relationship with your spouse. HomeBuilders Bible studies are designed to help you strengthen your marriage and family in many of these critical areas.

Part One: The Big Problem

One basic problem is at the heart of every other problem in every marriage, and it's a problem we can't help you fix. No matter how hard you try, this is one problem that is too big for you to deal with on your own.

The problem is separation from God. If you want to experience marriage the way it was designed to be, you need a vital relationship with the God who created you and offers you the power to live a life of joy and purpose.

And what separates us from God is one more problem—sin. Most of us have assumed throughout our lives that the term "sin" refers to a list of bad habits that everyone agrees are wrong. We try to deal with our sin problem by working hard to become better people. We read books to learn how to control our anger, or we resolve to stop cheating on our taxes.

But in our hearts, we know our sin problem runs much deeper than a list of bad habits. All of us have rebelled against God. We have ignored him and have decided to run our own lives in a way that makes sense to us. The Bible says that the God who created us wants us to follow his plan for our lives. But because of our sin problem, we think our ideas and plans are better than his.

- *"For all have sinned and fall short of the glory of God"* (Romans 3:23).

What does it mean to "fall short of the glory of God"? It means that none of us has trusted and treasured God the way we should. We have sought to satisfy ourselves with other things and have treated those things as more valuable than God. We have gone our own way. According to the Bible, we have to pay a penalty for our sin. We cannot simply do things the way we choose and hope it will all be OK with God. Following our own plan leads to our destruction.

- *"There is a way that seems right to a man, but in the end it leads to death"* (Proverbs 14:12).

- *"For the wages of sin is death"* (Romans 6:23a).

The penalty for sin is that we are forever separated from God's love. God is holy, and we are sinful. No matter how hard we try, we cannot come up with some plan, like living a good life or even trying to do what the Bible says, and hope that we can avoid the penalty.

God's Solution to Sin

Thankfully, God has a way to solve our dilemma. He became a man through the person of Jesus Christ. He lived a holy life, in perfect obedience to God's plan. He also willingly died on a cross to pay our penalty for sin. Then he proved that he is more powerful than sin or death by rising from the dead. He alone has the power to overrule the penalty for our sin.

- *"Jesus answered, 'I am the way and the truth and the life. No one comes to the Father except through me' "* (John 14:6).

- *"But God demonstrates his own love for us in this: While we were still sinners, Christ died for us"* (Romans 5:8).

- *"Christ died for our sins...he was buried...he was raised on the third day according to the Scriptures...he appeared to Peter, and then to the Twelve. After that, he appeared to more than five hundred"* (1 Corinthians 15:3-6).

- *"For the wages of sin is death, but the gift of God is eternal life in Christ Jesus our Lord"* (Romans 6:23).

The death of Jesus has fixed our sin problem. He has bridged the gap between God and us. He is calling all of us to come to him and to give up our own flawed plan for how to run our lives. He wants us to trust God and his plan.

Accepting God's Solution

If you agree that you are separated from God, he is calling you to confess your sins. All of us have made messes of our lives because we have stubbornly preferred our ideas and plans over his. As a result, we deserve to be cut off from God's love and his care for us. But God has promised that if we will agree that we have rebelled against his plan for us and have messed up our lives, he will forgive us and will fix our sin problem.

- *"Yet to all who received him, to those who believed in his name, he gave the right to become children of God"* (John 1:12).

- *"For it is by grace you have been saved, through*

faith—and this not from yourselves, it is the gift of God—not by works, so that no one can boast" (Ephesians 2:8-9).

When the Bible talks about receiving Christ, it means we acknowledge that we are sinners and that we can't fix the problem ourselves. It means we turn away from our sin. And it means we trust Christ to forgive our sins and to make us the kind of people he wants us to be. It's not enough to just intellectually believe that Christ is the Son of God. We must trust in him and his plan for our lives by faith, as an act of the will.

Are things right between you and God, with him and his plan at the center of your life? Or is life spinning out of control as you seek to make your way on your own?

You can decide today to make a change. You can turn to Christ and allow him to transform your life. All you need to do is to talk to him and tell him what is stirring in your mind and in your heart. If you've never done this before, consider taking the steps listed here:

- Do you agree that you need God? Tell God.

- Have you made a mess of your life by following your own plan? Tell God.

- Do you want God to forgive you? Tell God.

- Do you believe that Jesus' death on the cross and his resurrection from the dead gave him the power to fix your sin problem and to grant you the gift of eternal life? Tell God.

- Are you ready to acknowledge that God's plan for your life is better than any plan you could come up with? Tell God.

- Do you agree that God has the right to be the Lord and master of your life? Tell God.

> *"Seek the Lord while he may be found;*
> *call on him while he is near"*
> (Isaiah 55:6).

Following is a suggested prayer:

Lord Jesus, I need you. Thank you for dying on the cross for my sins. I receive you as my Savior and Lord. Thank you for forgiving my sins and giving me eternal life. Make me the kind of person you want me to be.

Does this prayer express the desire of your heart? If it does, pray it right now, and Christ will come into your life, as he promised.

Part Two: Living the Christian Life

For a person who is a follower of Christ—a Christian—the penalty for sin is paid in full. But the effect of sin continues throughout our lives.

- *"If we claim to be without sin, we deceive ourselves and the truth is not in us"* (1 John 1:8).

- *"For what I do is not the good I want to do; no, the evil I do not want to do—this I keep on doing"* (Romans 7:19).

The effects of sin carry over into our marriages as well. Even Christians struggle to maintain solid, God-honoring marriages. Most couples eventually realize that they can't do it on their own. But with God's help, they can succeed. The Holy Spirit can have a huge impact in the marriages of Christians who live constantly, moment by moment, under his gracious direction.

Self-Centered Christians

Many Christians struggle to live the Christian life in their own strength because they are not allowing God to control their lives. Their interests are self-directed, often resulting in failure and frustration.

- *"Brothers, I could not address you as spiritual but as worldly—mere infants in Christ. I gave you milk, not solid food, for you were not yet ready for it. Indeed, you are still not ready. You are still worldly. For since there is jealousy and quarreling among you, are you not worldly? Are you not acting like mere men?"* (1 Corinthians 3:1-3).

The self-centered Christian cannot experience the abundant and fruitful Christian life. Such people trust in their own efforts to live the Christian life: They are either uninformed about—or have forgotten—God's love, forgiveness, and power. This kind of Christian

- has an up-and-down spiritual experience.

- cannot understand himself—he wants to do what is right, but cannot.

- fails to draw upon the power of the Holy Spirit to live the Christian life.

Some or all of the following traits may characterize the Christian who does not fully trust God:

disobedience	plagued by impure thoughts
lack of love for God and others	jealous
	worrisome
inconsistent prayer life	easily discouraged, frustrated
lack of desire for Bible study	critical
legalistic attitude	lack of purpose

Note: The individual who professes to be a Christian but who continues to practice sin should realize that he may not be a Christian at all, according to Ephesians 5:5 and 1 John 2:3; 3:6, 9.

Spirit-Centered Christians

When a Christian puts Christ on the throne of his life, he yields to God's control. This Christian's interests are directed by the Holy Spirit, resulting in harmony with God's plan.

- *"But the fruit of the Spirit is love, joy, peace, patience, kindness, goodness, faithfulness, gentleness and self-control. Against such things there is no law"* (Galatians 5:22-23).

Jesus said:

- *"I have come that they may have life, and have it to the full"* (John 10:10b).

- *"I am the vine; you are the branches. If a man remains in me and I in him, he will bear much fruit; apart from me you can do nothing"* (John 15:5).

- *"But you will receive power when the Holy Spirit comes on you; and you will be my witnesses in Jerusalem, and in all Judea and Samaria, and to the ends of the earth"* (Acts 1:8).

The following traits result naturally from the Holy Spirit's work in our lives:

Christ centered	love
Holy Spirit empowered	joy
motivated to tell others about Jesus	peace
	patience
dedicated to prayer	kindness
student of God's Word	goodness
trusts God	faithfulness
obeys God	gentleness
	self-control

The degree to which these traits appear in a Christian's life and marriage depends upon the extent to which the Christian trusts the Lord with every detail of life, and upon that person's maturity in Christ. One who is only beginning to understand the ministry of the Holy Spirit should not be discouraged if he is not as fruitful as mature Christians who have known and experienced this truth for a longer period of time.

Giving God Control

Jesus promises his followers an abundant and fruitful life as they allow themselves to be directed and empowered by the Holy Spirit. As we give God control of our lives, Christ lives in and through us in the power of the Holy Spirit (John 15).

If you sincerely desire to be directed and empowered by God, you can turn your life over to the control of the Holy Spirit right now (Matthew 5:6; John 7:37-39).

First, confess your sins to God, agreeing with him that you want to turn from any past sinful patterns in your life. Thank God in faith that he has forgiven all of your sins because Christ died for you (Colossians 2:13-15; 1 John 1:9; 2:1-3; Hebrews 10:1-18).

Be sure to offer every area of your life to God (Romans 12:1-2). Consider what areas you might rather keep to yourself, and be sure you're willing to give God control in those areas.

By faith, commit yourself to living according to the Holy Spirit's guidance and power.

- *Live by the Spirit:* **"So I say, live by the Spirit, and you will not gratify the desires of the sinful nature. For the sinful nature desires what is contrary to the Spirit, and the Spirit what is contrary to the sinful nature. They are in conflict with each other, so that you do not do what you want"** (Galatians 5:16-17).

- *Trust in God's promise:* **"This is the confidence we have in approaching God: that if we ask anything according to his will, he hears us. And if we know that he hears us—whatever we ask—we know that we have what we asked of him"** (1 John 5:14-15).

Expressing Your Faith Through Prayer

Prayer is one way of expressing your faith to God. If the prayer that follows expresses your sincere desire, consider praying the prayer or putting the thoughts into your own words:

> **Dear God, I need you. I acknowledge that I have been directing my own life and that, as a result, I have sinned against you. I thank you that you have forgiven my sins through Christ's death on the cross for me. I now invite Christ to take his place on the throne of my life. Take control of my life through the Holy Spirit as you promised you would if I asked in faith. I now thank you for directing my life and for empowering me through the Holy Spirit.**

Walking in the Spirit

If you become aware of an area of your life (an attitude or an action) that is displeasing to God, simply confess your sin, and thank God that he has forgiven your sins on the basis of Christ's death on the cross. Accept God's love and forgiveness by faith, and continue to have fellowship with him.

If you find that you've taken back control of your life through sin—a definite act of disobedience—try this exercise, "Spiritual Breathing," as you give that control back to God.

1. Exhale. Confess your sin. Agree with God that you've sinned against him, and thank him for his forgiveness of it, according to 1 John 1:9 and Hebrews 10:1-25. Remember that confession involves repentance, a determination to change attitudes and actions.

2. Inhale. Surrender control of your life to Christ, inviting the Holy Spirit to once again take charge. Trust that he now directs and empowers you, according to the command of Galatians 5:16-17 and the promise of 1 John 5:14-15. Returning to your faith in God enables you to continue to experience God's love and forgiveness.

Revolutionizing Your Marriage

This new commitment of your life to God will enrich your marriage. Sharing with your spouse what you've committed to is a powerful step in solidifying this commitment. As you exhibit the Holy Spirit's work within you, your spouse may be drawn to make the same commitment you've made. If both of you have given control of your lives to the Holy Spirit, you'll be able to help each other remain true to God, and your marriage may be revolutionized. With God in charge of your lives, life becomes an amazing adventure.

Leader Notes

Contents

About Leading a HomeBuilders Group

What is the leader's job?

Your role is that of "facilitator"—one who encourages people to think and to discover what Scripture says, who helps group members feel comfortable, and who keeps things moving forward.

What is the best setting and time schedule for this study?

This study is designed as a small-group home Bible study. However, it can be adapted for use in a Sunday school setting as well. Here are some suggestions for using this study in a small group and in a Sunday school class:

In a small group

To create a friendly and comfortable atmosphere, it is recommended that you do this study in a home setting. In many cases, the couple that leads the study also serves as host to the group. Sometimes involving another couple as host is a good idea. Choose the option you believe will work best for your group, taking into account factors such as the number of couples participating and the location.

Each session is designed as a ninety-minute study, but we recommend a two-hour block of time. This will allow you to move through each part of the study at a more relaxed pace. However, be sure to keep in mind one of the cardinal rules of a small group: Good groups start *and* end on time. People's time is valuable, and your group will appreciate your being respectful of this.

In a Sunday school class

There are two important adaptations you need to make if you

want to use this study in a class setting: (1) The material you cover should focus on the content from the Blueprints section of each session. Blueprints is the heart of each session and is designed to last sixty minutes. (2) Most Sunday school classes are taught in a teacher format instead of a small-group format. If this study will be used in a class setting, the class should adapt to a small-group dynamic. This will involve an interactive, discussion-based format and may also require a class to break into multiple smaller groups (we recommend groups of six to eight people).

What is the best size group?

We recommend from four to eight couples (including you and your spouse). If you have more people interested than you think you can accommodate, consider asking someone else to lead a second group. If you have a large group, you are encouraged at various times in the study to break into smaller subgroups. This helps you cover the material in a timely fashion and allows for optimum interaction and participation within the group.

What about refreshments?

Many groups choose to serve refreshments, which help create an environment of fellowship. If you plan on including refreshments in your study, here are a couple of suggestions: (1) For the first session (or two) you should provide the refreshments and then allow the group to be involved by having people sign up to bring them on later dates. (2) Consider starting your group with a short time of informal fellowship and refreshments (fifteen minutes), then move into the study. If couples are late, they miss only the food and don't disrupt the study. You may also want to have refreshments available at the end of your meeting to encourage fellowship, but remember, respect the group members' time by ending the study on schedule and allowing anyone who needs to leave right away the opportunity to do so gracefully.

What about child care?

Groups handle this differently depending on their needs. Here are a couple of options you may want to consider:

- Have group members be responsible for making their own arrangements.
- As a group, hire child care, and have all the kids watched in one location.

What about prayer?

An important part of a small group is prayer. However, as the leader, you need to be sensitive to the level of comfort the people in your group have toward praying in front of others. Never call on people to pray aloud if you don't know if they are comfortable doing this. There are a number of creative approaches you can take, such as modeling prayer, calling for volunteers, and letting people state their prayers in the form of finishing a sentence. A tool that is helpful in a group is a prayer list. You are encouraged to utilize a prayer list, but let it be someone else's ministry to the group. You should lead the prayer time, but allow another couple in the group the opportunity to create, update, and distribute prayer lists.

In closing

An excellent resource that covers leading a HomeBuilders group in greater detail is the *HomeBuilders Leader Guide* by Drew and Kit Coons. This book may be obtained at your local Christian bookstore or by contacting Group Publishing or FamilyLife.

About the Leader Notes

The sessions in this study can be easily led without a lot of preparation time. However, accompanying Leader Notes have been provided to assist you in preparation. The categories within the Leader Notes are as follows:

Objectives

The purpose of the Objectives is to help focus on the issues that will be presented in each session.

Notes and Tips

This section will relate any general comments about the session. This information should be viewed as ideas, helps, and suggestions. You may want to create a checklist of things you want to be sure to do in each session.

Commentary

Included in this section are notes that relate specifically to Blueprints questions. Not all Blueprints questions in each session will have accompanying commentary notes. Questions with related commentaries are designated by numbers (for example, Blueprints question 3 in Session One would correspond to number 3 in the Commentary section of Session One Leader Notes).

Session One:
What Legacy Are You Leaving?

Objectives

Your life will have an impact for generations to come.

In this session parents will

- reflect on the legacy others have left in their lives.
- acknowledge the importance of character in the legacy they leave.
- recognize that character must be based on God and his Word.

Notes and Tips

1. Welcome to the first session of the HomeBuilders course *Building Character in Your Children.* While it is anticipated that most of the participants in this HomeBuilders Parenting Series study will be couples with children, be aware that you may have single parents, future parents, or even one parent from a marriage participating. Welcome everyone warmly, and work to create a supportive and encouraging environment.

You'll find certain features throughout this study that are specifically geared toward couples, such as designated couples questions and the HomeBuilders Projects. However, we encourage you as the leader to be flexible and sensitive to your group. For example, if you have a single parent in your group, you might invite that person to join you and your spouse when a couple's question is indicated in the study.

Or, if there are multiple single parents, you may want to encourage them to join together for these questions. Likewise, for the HomeBuilders Project at the end of every session, you may want to encourage singles to complete what they can individually or to work with another single parent on the project.

2. If you have not already done so, you will want to read the "About the Sessions" information on pages 4 and 5, as well as "About Leading a HomeBuilders Group" and "About the Leader Notes" starting on page 122.

3. As part of the first session, review with the group some Ground Rules (see page 11 in the Introduction).

4. Be sure you have a study guide for each person. You'll also want to have extra Bibles and pens or pencils.

5. Depending on the size of your group, you may spend longer than fifteen minutes on the Warm-Up section. If this happens, try to finish the Blueprints section in forty-five to sixty minutes. It is a good idea to mark the questions in Blueprints that you want to be sure to cover. Encourage couples to look at any questions you don't get to during the session when they do the HomeBuilders Project for this session. And be sure to allow enough time at the end to do the Wrap-Up activity, as couples will be referring back to this during this session's HomeBuilders Project.

6. You will notice a note in the margin at the start of the Blueprints section that recommends breaking into smaller groups. The reason for this is twofold: (1) to help facilitate discussion and participation by everyone, and (2) to help you be able to get through the material in the allotted time.

7. Throughout the sessions in this course, you will find questions that are designed for spouses to answer together (like question 7 in this session). The purpose of these "couples questions" is to foster communication and unity between spouses and give couples an opportunity to deal with personal issues. While couples are free to share their responses to these questions with the group, respect that not all couples will want to do so.

8. With this group just getting under way, it's not too late to invite another couple to join the group. During Wrap-Up, challenge everyone to think about someone they could invite to the next session.

9. Before dismissing, make a special point to tell the group about the importance of the HomeBuilders Project. Encourage each couple to "Make a Date" before the next meeting to complete this session's project. Mention that you'll ask about their experience with the project at the next session.

In addition to the HomeBuilders Projects, there are six Parent-Child Interactions (starting on page 93). These are designed to help give parents an opportunity to communicate with their children. Though we recommend that parents try and complete the interactions between sessions, we know this will be a challenge. We encourage couples to place a priority on first completing the HomeBuilders Projects and then doing the Parent-Child Interactions when they have time, whether between sessions or at a later date.

10. To conclude this first session, you may want to offer a closing prayer instead of asking others to pray aloud. Many people are uncomfortable praying in front of others, and unless you already know your group well, it may be wise to slowly venture into various methods of prayer.

Commentary

Here's some additional information related to select Blueprints questions. The numbers that follow correspond to the

Blueprints questions of the same numbers in the session. Notes are not included for every question, as many of the questions in this study are designed for group members to draw from their own opinions and experiences. If you share any of these points, be sure to do so in a manner that does not stifle discussion by making you the authority with the "real answers." Keep in mind that these sessions are designed around group interaction and participation.

3. All parents leave some type of legacy to their children, sometimes in ways they barely recognize. Sometimes this legacy consists of material things, but the most important legacy is left in the hearts and minds of their children. The way you treat your children—what you say and what you do—will impact them. They will follow your example in the way you treat your spouse, the way you interact with other people, the choices you make.

Sometimes a legacy is negative. A parent who abandons his or her children can leave a harmful legacy of fear and doubt in the mind of a child.

8. True wisdom and character come from a relationship with God.

9. The most important thing we can give our children is encouragement to put their faith and trust in God. Each generation is responsible to tell the next about who God is and what God has done for us.

10. There is ample historical evidence to show that the founders of the United States knew and feared God. Many of them were ordained ministers. And for most of our nation's history, our people have made their faith in God the foundation of our culture. In recent decades, new generations have grown up without knowledge of God and are rejecting God. We have become callous and insensitive to the demands and expectations of God—purity, justice, a disdain for sin, and charity to the poor. We view church attendance as a social option rather than a needed spiritual endeavor. We no longer view the fear of God as foundational to social behavior. We have become much like the parents that are written about in Psalm 78.

11. It is a person's character that, in the long run, determines his or her true success or failure. Each year we see new examples of rich, talented, and powerful men and women who become caught in scandals. It can happen to anyone with weak character.

Attention HomeBuilders Leaders

FamilyLife invites you to register your HomeBuilders group. Your registration connects you to the HomeBuilders Leadership Network, a worldwide movement of couples who are using HomeBuilders to strengthen marriages and families in their communities. You'll receive the latest news about HomeBuilders and other ministry opportunities to help strengthen marriages and families in your community. As the HomeBuilders Leadership Network grows, we'll offer additional resources such as online training, prayer requests, and chats with authors. There's no cost or obligation to register; simply go to www.familylife.com/homebuilders.

Session Two:
The Foundation for Character

Objectives

The key components that establish the foundation of God-honoring character are a relationship with Christ and obedience to God's Word.

In this session parents will

- consider the connection between character and an ongoing relationship with Christ.
- discuss the need for obedience to God's Word.
- share ideas for teaching our children about God's Word and modeling God-honoring character to them.

Notes and Tips

1. Because this is the second session, your group members have probably warmed up to one another but may not yet feel free to be completely open about their relationships. Don't force the issue. Continue to encourage couples to attend and to complete the projects.

2. If new people join the group this session, during Warm-Up ask them to introduce themselves to the group and to share the names and ages of their children. Also give a brief summary of the main points from Session One, and have the group pass around their books to record contact information (page 14).

3. Make sure the arrangements for refreshments (if you're planning to have them) are covered.

4. If your group has decided to use a prayer list (which we highly recommend), make sure this is covered.

5. If you told the group during the first session that you'd be asking them about the first HomeBuilders Project, be sure to do so. This is an opportunity to establish an environment of accountability. And be prepared to share a report of your own.

6. For Extra Impact: Here's a suggestion for a more active Warm-Up dealing with the subject of peer pressure. At the start of the meeting, ask for a volunteer who is willing to be part of an experiment, and then have this person leave the room for a short time. When that person is out of the room, decide as a group what you want to try and get this person to do when he or she returns—via peer pressure. For example, you may as a group try and get this person to sing, tell a joke, show off a dance move, anything that would be in the spirit of fun. The goal is not to embarrass this person, but rather to try and demonstrate the power of peer pressure. After spending a couple of minutes trying to persuade the person to do what you came up with, take a few minutes to discuss this experiment. Ask the volunteer to share how he or she felt, and likewise, ask the group what it was like to be on the side of trying to pressure someone to do something. Then close by asking: How does your relationship with Christ help you maintain God-honoring character in the face of pressures from the world?

7. This session talks about an ongoing relationship with Christ as a key foundation of character. It's possible that not everyone in your group may know or understand what it means to be a Christian. Pray for discernment. It may be helpful for you to be prepared to briefly share about your relationship with Christ during the Wrap-Up. We have also included an article (starting on page 108), "Our Problems, God's Answers" that you can direct people to as well.

Commentary

Note: The numbers that follow correspond to the Blueprints questions of the same numbers in the session.

1. Alex appeared to have the trappings of Christianity but not the real thing. He ignored the need to establish and develop a personal relationship with Christ.

3. First and foremost, live a vital, growing Christian life before your children. Let them see you daily seeking the Lord. It's also important to set an example in confessing sins, asking for forgiveness, and making restitution. All three of these are steps to true repentance. Children need to know and see their parents take a stand for righteousness even when it involves the possibility of being misunderstood or rejected.

6. The Word of God provides truth and direction in a world of darkness.

7. They can easily become selfish and self-centered. They will not know or care that there are principles of right and wrong on which society is built.

Session Three:
Your Family's Character

Objectives

You can encourage God-honoring character in your children by establishing it in the environment of your home.

In this session parents will

- examine the concept of a family reputation.
- analyze how people view their own families.
- decide the values they want to stand for and emphasize with their children.

Notes and Tips

1. Remember the importance of starting and ending on time.

2. As an example to the group, it is important that you and your spouse complete the HomeBuilders Project each session.

3. Question 10 in Blueprints calls for couples to look up different Scripture passages. This approach allows the group to simultaneously examine multiple passages, saving time and giving group members an opportunity to learn from each other.

4. During Wrap-Up, make a point to encourage couples to "Make a Date" to complete the HomeBuilders Project for this session.

5. You may find it helpful to make some notes right after the meeting to help you evaluate how this session went. Ask yourself questions such as: "Did everyone participate? Is there anyone I need to make a special effort to follow up with before the next session?"

Commentary

Note: The numbers that follow correspond to the Blueprints questions of the same numbers in the session.

1. This question could also be looked at from the flip side: What is a business or organization in the community with "a reputation," and how was this negative image created? Did it happen overnight, or was it gradual? Explain.

A word of caution: while negative examples can also be instructive, be careful to keep the conversation constructive.

3. The reality is that there are families with both positive and negative reputations. Both of these examples can be instructive to us in evaluating our own families. However, similar to the word of caution under note 1, be diligent to keep the discussion moving in a positive and constructive direction. You never know who might be someone else's friend or relative.

7. A family characterized by serving God will be a family that applies Scripture in their relationships. For example, if you want 1 Peter 3:8-10 to be applied in your family relationships, you need to model the right response to your children of how to respond when someone insults or hurts you. When one child wants to seek revenge on another for a hurtful comment or action, you would show the child how to respond with a blessing instead.

Session Four:
The Enemy of Character

Objectives

Our natural foolishness hinders any effort to build God-honoring character.

In this session parents will

- contrast the differences between the wise and the foolish in Scripture.
- discuss the natural tendency of children toward foolishness.
- talk about practical ways to drive foolishness out of children.

Notes and Tips

1. By this time, group members should be getting more comfortable with each other. For prayer at the end of this session, you may want to give everyone an opportunity to pray by asking the group to finish a sentence that goes something like this: "Lord, I want to thank you for..." Be sensitive to anyone who may not feel comfortable doing this.

   Congratulations! You are halfway through this study. It's time for a checkup: How's the group going? What has worked well so far? What things might you consider changing as you approach this and the remaining sessions?

2. For the Wrap-Up, if the group as a whole is small enough, and if there seems to be general agreement on which items from the created list present the greatest challenges, conduct the follow-up discussion all together. However, an

option to consider—especially if you have a large group, or if there is a wide diversity of opinion on which items from the group's list are most challenging, is to have the follow-up discussion be done in pairs as couples.

Commentary

Note: The numbers that follow correspond to the Blueprints questions of the same numbers in the session.

1. We define a fool as a person who refuses to live and behave in light of what he or she knows is right and becomes a willing slave of his impulses.

2. Children often act foolishly because they do not have the knowledge or experience to know that what they are doing will have undesirable consequences. Adults often act foolishly even though they are fully aware that their actions will lead to consequences.

4. Some people don't want to grow up and give up their freedom, their fun, or their vices. Some people are so selfish that they continue to make foolish choices most of their lives.

8. One suggestion would be to separate the offending child from the child that was verbally hurt or attacked. Do not let them play together or be together for two or more hours. Sit down and talk with the offending child, and ask the child how it would feel if someone said the hurtful thing that was said to him or her.

9. In a sense, the old adage "practice makes perfect" applies here. Practice in saying no, both rehearsed and live, shows your children that they can avoid giving in to foolish impulses. They also experience the blessings of good choices.

11. Fools don't want to be told they are wrong. They don't want to be under the authority of another person. They don't want to feel like anyone is infringing on their personal freedom.

Session Five:
Keeping Our Character

Objectives

Character is built during times of testing.

In this session parents will

- examine how times of testing and suffering affect our character.
- discuss the need to be lights in a culture of darkness.
- share experiences of trials and how these tested their relationship with God.

Notes and Tips

1. **For Extra Impact:** To put a little different twist on the Warm-Up, experience darkness as a group instead of just talking about it. Adapt the first two steps from the Parent-Child Interaction 5: Living in Darkness (page 101) for your group. After doing those steps, discuss the final bullet point question in the Warm-Up exercise.

2. Due to the subject in this session, it is quite possible that discussion on various Blueprints questions will run long. Be sensitive not to stifle good discussion; however, try and politely keep things moving along as well. You may want to mark ahead of time the questions you want to be sure to cover. It is also important in this session for the group to do the Wrap-Up, as this exercise will come into play during this session's HomeBuilders Project. If there are questions you end up not covering during the session, encourage couples to go back and look at these as a couple when they do this session's project.

3. You and your spouse may want to consider writing notes of thanks and encouragement to the members of your group this week. Thank them for their commitment and contribution to the group, and let them know that you're praying for them. (Make a point to pray from them as you write their notes.)

4. Looking ahead: For the next session—the last one of this course—you may want to ask a person or a couple to share what this course or group has meant to him or her. This could be done during either the Warm-Up or Wrap-Up time.

Commentary

3. Jesus is the source of spiritual knowledge and revelation about God the Father and Creator. He enlightens people to the knowledge and person of God.

Note: The numbers that follow correspond to the Blueprints questions of the same numbers in the session.

5. We are to emulate Jesus Christ. We are to be a light that reveals God— or more accurately, Jesus Christ as the Son of God. We should show the love, the righteousness, the compassion, and the provision of God to others.

6. This is one of the great challenges of the Christian life—to be close enough to the world to show people there is a significant difference in our lifestyle and theirs. It is a daily challenge that can only be met through the grace of God manifested in us. We must allow God to love through us. We must pray for those around us. We must meet the physical needs of those around us. We must love our families and church members unconditionally. We must guide and train our families to love each other and those around them.

7. Only by the grace of God. And under God's grace, we need to grow in our knowledge of God and his Word so that we have an intimate understanding of how God wants us to live. God's Word answers many questions about how we should live and how we should teach our children. We must be living examples of Christ if we are to teach our children to do the same. They will watch and catch our convictions and beliefs much faster if they see us live them out in daily life. We must show them how we make choices about what we allow ourselves to view or hear in today's culture. We must show them how we respond to those who do not share our faith. We must show them how to speak up for Christ and reach out to tell others about how to know Jesus.

8. During trials we often must learn to depend entirely on God, leaning on the Bible and prayer. Our entire view of God is tested: Do we truly believe God is who he says? Do we truly believe the Bible is true? Do we have faith to accept that God knows what is best for us; that he gives us the strength and comfort to endure?

10. Trials and problems strengthen our faith far more than times of peace and abundance. It is in those times we learn to trust God.

11. We must learn to call out to God and focus on him. Seeking God and living to please him in times of trial, testing, or temptation is the best solution to getting through what we face.

Session Six:
Modeling Character

Objectives

You are the primary example your children have for what kind of person they should become.

In this session parents will

- acknowledge the importance of modeling the character we want to be part of our children.
- recognize different areas in which we need to model God-honoring character.
- reflect on what they've learned from participating in this study.

Notes and Tips

1. While this HomeBuilders study has great value, people are likely to return to previous patterns of living unless they commit to a plan for carrying on the progress they've made. During this final session of the course, encourage couples to take specific steps beyond this series to continue to strengthen their marriage and family. For example, you may want to challenge couples who have developed the habit of a "date night" during the course of this study to continue this practice. Also, you may want the group to consider doing another HomeBuilders study. Call attention to page 107 in the "Where Do We Go From Here?" section during the Wrap-Up.

2. **For Extra Impact:** Here's a suggestion for making the closing prayer time special. Have the group form a prayer

circle. Then have each person or couple, if comfortable doing so, take a turn standing or kneeling in the middle of the circle while the group prays specifically for that person or couple.

3. As a part of this last session, devote time for planning one more meeting—a party to celebrate the completion of this study!

Commentary

Note: The numbers that follow correspond to the Blueprints questions of the same numbers in the session.

1. It is evident that Paul not only told the Thessalonians how to live for Christ, but he also showed them. They "worked night and day" among the Thessalonians; they were "holy, righteous, and blameless." They encouraged and comforted them as parents would with children.

2. This reveals a level of intimate involvement—sharing their life experience with the Thessalonians.

3. Both are important, but the model you set in front of your children may influence them the most. In ways you and they may never fully understand, they will pattern their lives after yours.

5. We become a witness to how God will answer our prayers by how we respond, answer, and keep our word to our children.

7. We may have difficulty asking our children for forgiveness because we think that asking forgiveness for wrong attitudes or words somehow shows that we are weak, or proves that we were wrong in our correction, or perhaps our pride prevents us from making this request.

10. In speech: Guarding what we say and resisting angry outbursts.

BUILDING CHARACTER IN YOUR CHILDRE

In life: By seeking God's guidance daily and in major decisions.

In love: By loving our children unconditionally, and by loving the unlovely—the homeless, the poor.

In faith: By turning to God in prayer during both difficult times and in daily life.

In purity: Guarding what we watch, what we see, and what we gaze on.

Prayer Requests

Prayer Requests

Does Your Church Offer Marriage Insurance?

Great marriages don't just happen—husbands and wives need to nurture them. They need to make their marriage relationship a priority.

That's where the HomeBuilders Couples Series® can help! The series consists of interactive 6- to 7-week small group studies that make it easy for couples to really open up with each other. The result is fun, non-threatening interactions that build stronger Christ-centered relationships between spouses—and with other couples!

Whether you've been married for years or are newly married, this series will help you and your spouse discover timeless principles from God's Word that you can apply to your marriage and make it the best it can be!

The HomeBuilders Leader Guide gives you all the information and encouragement you need to start and lead a dynamic HomeBuilders small group.

The HomeBuilders Couples Series includes these life-changing studies:

- Building Teamwork in Your Marriage
- Building Your Marriage *(also available in Spanish!)*
- Building Your Mate's Self-Esteem
- Growing Together in Christ
- Improving Communication in Your Marriage *(also available in Spanish!)*
- Making Your Remarriage Last
- Mastering Money in Your Marriage
- Overcoming Stress in Your Marriage
- Resolving Conflict in Your Marriage

And check out the HomeBuilders Parenting Series!

- Building Character in Your Children
- Establishing Effective Discipline for Your Children
- Guiding Your Teenagers

- Helping Your Children Know God
- Improving Your Parenting
- Raising Children of Faith

Look for the **HomeBuilders Couples Series and HomeBuilders Parenting Series** at your favorite Christian supplier or write:

FAMILYLIFE™
Bringing Timeless Principles Home

www.familylife.com

P.O. Box 485, Loveland, CO 80539-0485.
www.grouppublishing.com